CARL LEWIS

CARL LEWIS
LEGEND CHASER

Nathan Aaseng

Lerner Publications Company ■ Minneapolis

To Ed Belka and Steve Hay

LIBRARY OF CONGRESS CATALOGING IN PUBLICATION DATA

Aaseng, Nathan.
 Carl Lewis: legend chaser.

 (The Achievers)
 Summary: A biography of Carl Lewis, the man who broke
Jesse Owens' record by winning four gold medals in track
and field in the 1984 Olympic games.

 1. Lewis, Carl, 1961-   —Juvenile literature. 2. Track
and field athletes—United States—Biography—Juvenile literature. [1. Lewis, Carl, 1961-   . 2. Track and field athletes]
I. Title. II. Series.

GV697.L48A23   1985 796.4'2'0924 [B] [92]   84-23348
ISBN 0-8225-0496-0 (lib. bdg.)

Manufactured in the United States of America

International Standard Book Number: 0-8225-0496-0
Library of Congress Catalog Card Number: 84-23348

3   4   5   6   7   8   9   10   94   93   92   91   90   89   88   87

CARL LEWIS

The lean figure at the end of the runway tried to calm his angry nerves. These were the Olympic Games, and soon it would be his moment to take center stage. With his thoughts focused on simply doing his best, he had no idea that he was about to be at the center of a freak moment in sports history.

But conditions were all coming together for him at just the right time. All that lay between the takeoff board and the end of the long-jump pit was the thin air of Mexico City. At such a high altitude, the air would give less resistance to his jump than at lower elevations. And there was a gentle tailwind that would push him slightly through the air. At the time of his jump, this breeze would reach two meters per second (4.47 miles per hour). If it increased even slightly, the jump would be considered wind-aided, and it would not count as a world record.

Bob Beamon would not have been the logical choice for this historic moment. He was a good jumper, but he did not rank with the greatest. During these 1968 Olympics, he had barely dodged disaster and had qualified for the finals only on his last preliminary jump. There were many other jumpers with better form who were more consistent than Bob. While others pranced down the runway with carefully measured strides, Beamon was not always sure whether he would be jumping off his left foot or his right.

Fifteen world records in track and field, including Bob Beamon's legendary long jump, were set in this Mexico City stadium during the 1968 Olympic Games.

Beamon soars high over the heads of Olympic officials on his "impossible" gold-medal-winning jump.

Now it was time for Beamon to jump. When he tore off down the runway, he seemed to be driven by an extra burst of energy. After running faster than he had ever before in his life, Bob hit his takeoff perfectly and soared. He didn't splash into the sand until he was dangerously near the end of the pit. Aware of what had happened, the crowd screamed its approval. When he heard that his distance had been 8.9 meters, Beamon clapped his hands over his eyes, collapsed, and kissed the ground.

In the words of a competitor, Beamon had "destroyed the event." Knowing their best efforts would look foolish compared to Beamon's, the rest of the jumpers could hardly fire up for their turns. The United States' jumper had sailed 29 feet, 2-½ inches, almost 2 *feet* beyond the old world record! Some called it the greatest achievement in athletic history and predicted the record would last well into the next century.

Three years later, a 10-year-old boy took a tape measure out into his yard. Stretching out the tape, he carefully measured 29 feet, 2-½ inches on the grass. Young Carl Lewis looked from one end of the mark to the other, eyes huge with wonder that a human could jump so far. Although he did not realize it, Carl was sizing up the task that was in front of him. In 10 years, he would begin a relentless assault on that "untouchable" record.

Several years later, Carl met his dad's hero, Jesse Owens. The Buckeye Bullet from Ohio State University had been the greatest track and field star in United States' history. It was Owens who had shocked Adolph Hitler's powerful German team in the 1936 Olympics by winning four gold medals in track and field. As he shook hands with the great Owens, Lewis stared into the face of a second legend. No man had ever challenged Owens' record of four gold medals in

Jesse Owens on the victory stand after taking another gold medal in the 1936 Olympics

track and field in one Olympics. Like the legendary jump of Bob Beamon, the legend of Jesse Owens was so great that only Carl Lewis would consider going after it.

If a mad scientist tried to use principles of inherited traits to create a spectacular sprinter and leaper, he might well have considered pairing a couple from Tuskegee Institute in Alabama. Evelyn Lawler was ahead of her time in women's sports. She devoted full effort to such activities as basketball and track and had placed sixth in the hurdles during the 1951 Pan American Games. Had it not been for an injury,

Carl inherited grace, speed, and skill from his mother, one of Tuskegee Institute's finest athletes.

Bill Lewis played
football at Tuskegee.

Lawler would have had a good chance of competing
in the 1952 Olympics. The man she married, William
McKinley Lewis, played football and competed in the
sprints and the long jump for Tuskegee. Both enjoyed
athletics so much that they planned to make careers
out of coaching and teaching physical education.

A Hollywood writer dreaming up a birthplace for
the person who would challenge Jesse Owens might

place him in Owens' home state of Alabama. Carl Lewis, in fact, was born in Alabama, the third of the Lewis' four children. At the age of two, Carl went along with his family to Willingboro, New Jersey, where his parents had found jobs teaching and coaching for rival high schools.

Bill and Evelyn Lewis cared so much about their favorite sport, track and field, that they used their own money to organize a track club in Willingboro. The four Lewis children all benefited from their

Carl hoped to reward his mother (*above*) and other family members for their coaching and encouragement by winning four gold medals in the 1984 Olympics.

parents' dedication to sports. Although they were never pushed into competing, they were influenced by their parents' enthusiasm. Mackie, the oldest, was a sprinter who set a county record for the 220-yard dash. Cleve polished his skills in soccer so well that he became the first American black ever drafted by the pros and played two seasons with the Memphis Rogues.

Carol, a year younger than Carl, seemed to be the best athlete of all. Blessed with a limitless supply of energy, she kept up with Carl so well that her brother included her as one of his gang. Her excellent coordination and fearless nature combined to scare her parents half to death. She and Carl would try nearly any running, climbing, or jumping trick, regardless of the risk. Carl and Carol hung closely together all through childhood. When Carl began taking cello lessons, Carol started right in on the violin. When their parents headed out to the track, Carl and Carol tagged along to play in the sand of the long-jump pit.

Carl first became interested in jumping at age nine when his dad brought home a load of sand for a patio foundation. In the minds of the Lewis children, sand was for jumping, and they made their own long-jump pit out of the patio sand. Soon even the beach became their glorified long-jump pit. Carl and Carol

Carl's sister, Carol (*above*), also an outstanding athlete, was expected to challenge for a medal in the women's long jump in the 1984 Olympics but failed to qualify for the finals.

would carefully build sand castles and then back off and take running leaps to smash them.

Hurdles, too, were a basic toy for the Lewis family. Carl and Carol would often set up a course of makeshift hurdles in their back yard. One problem that arose, however, was that Carl was not the athlete

14

Carol was. Small for his age, he frequently lost when racing his younger sister.

Privately, Bill and Evelyn thought Carl might be the non-athlete of the family. For the most part, he could handle his defeats without bitterness. But every so often, his resentment came to the surface. "I'm tired of losing," he once complained to his dad. He was told that he would just have to work harder at winning or else quit.

So Carl continued to plug away at sports, especially long jumping. Long jumping doesn't normally attract many young children, and it was the unpopularity of the sport that appealed to Carl. Instead of waiting his turn to practice with a mob of sprinters, Carl could practice long jumping without having to take turns. In a way, it was twice as fun as sprinting because a long jumper got to sprint *and* jump on the same turn.

Only in the Lewis family could a boy like Carl have been considered a non-athlete. By the end of the ninth grade, he was jumping 22 feet, a mark that few high school seniors can reach. He was gaining that distance with his remarkable jumping form, however, not with outstanding speed or strength, and his times in the sprints and hurdles were nothing outstanding. Meanwhile, Carl's refusal to listen to coaches made going much farther in sports doubtful.

15

Nature then stepped in to change Carl's life completely, and he started to gain the inches and muscles that he needed to improve his performances. After sprouting nearly three inches during one year in high school, Carl no longer lost races. He owned a best time of 10.6 seconds in the 100-yard dash at the start of his junior year, and, with his new size and strength, immediately dropped that to an eye-catching 9.8. Now Carl wanted to concentrate on sprinting and drop the hurdles. "Fine," said his coach. "If you can get your 100 time down to 9.5, you won't have to run any more hurdles." By the end of the season, Lewis had sped through a race in 9.3!

In the long jump, however, Carl ran into problems more serious than occasional squabbles with coaches. While he was steadily improving his distances, he was just as steadily ruining his career. Carl's style of jumping high in the air put far too much strain on his leg. While still in high school, his knees swelled up so badly that he had to skip practices. He could still get some remarkable jumps on those knees during meets, but there was a danger he could cause more serious damage to them. True, he could set an American high school record of 26 feet, 8 inches, and he did finish third in the 1979 Pan American Games. But would his legs last long enough for him to reach his tremendous potential?

By now, Lewis had made up his mind to try to zero in on the feats of those two track legends, Beamon and Owens. As part of his plan, he enrolled at the University of Houston. There he would come under the guidance of Tom Tellez, one of track's most knowledgeable coaches. The combination of a tough-minded coach and a notoriously independent athlete seemed dangerous, and some of Carl's high school coaches might have expected that situation to explode.

Tellez seemed to be asking for trouble when he told Carl to scrap the jumping style he had spent years perfecting. Even the most coachable athletes often have trouble getting used to changing their routines, especially if they have been successful. And Lewis had turned his back on advice far less drastic than what Tellez was suggesting.

All Carl needed, however, was to be told *why* he should do something. And Tellez had the knowledge to explain *why* Carl's leg wouldn't hold up to the strain of being slammed down at high speed. The coach showed how Carl's problem was made worse by his attempts to get high in the air on his jumps. Tellez insisted that speed was far more important than height in gaining distance. Since Carl was an excellent sprinter, he had an advantage over other jumpers, and Tellez said he should learn to use it.

The first step in improving Lewis' jumping was to have him *stop* jumping. During his freshman year at Houston, Carl was told to work on his sprinting and leave long jumping alone. Only when his leg had fully healed was Lewis allowed to practice and to try out Tellez' new jumping methods. To get an idea of how hard it is for a trained athlete to start over with a new technique, imagine relearning to tie your shoes using only your thumbs and smallest fingers. An athlete who was content with being one of the best would probably not bother trying to change. But an athlete who was chasing legends as Lewis was would try almost anything to succeed.

As it turned out, there was a great deal more to Carl Lewis than just natural speed and spring. He was also, in his coach's words, "a physical genius." All Tellez had to do was to explain the mechanics of what needed to be done—such as how the arms and legs should be carried and what angle his take-off should take—and Carl was able to do it right the first time. First, Carl had to learn to practice only *part* of the long jump at a time. His own injuries were proof of the surprising danger in what seemed to be a very simple exercise. A world-class long jumper may reach a speed greater than 25 miles per hour during his approach, and even the most experienced long jumper feels nervous when he plants his foot for the takeoff at that speed. The impact can be brutal, as Carl once showed when he sheared two metal spikes off his shoe during a jump! Some doctors worried that if Lewis ever hit the takeoff board at his absolute top speed, the impact could destroy his leg. For this reason, Carl rarely took a full running jump in practice. If he were to jump at all, he would take only a short run before jumping.

Much of Lewis' practice time was spent in simply striding down the runway. Since all long jumps are measured from the end of the takeoff board, success depends on making sure the jumping foot always lands as near to the end of the board as possible. For example, if a jumper takes off 10 inches behind the board, he or she must actually sail 27 feet and *10 inches* in order to get credit for a 27-foot jump. But if even a sliver of the foot touches beyond the board, a foul is declared, and the jump is not measured. Carl spent countless hours working on his stride so that even at high speed he could almost automatically jump at precisely the spot he wanted. With the help of his coach, Carl found he could work up to his best long-jumping speed in 23 strides. Time after time, he practiced speeding down the runway so that in those 23 strides he would travel exactly 168 feet. (Later he changed to 171-foot run so he could use slightly longer strides.)

Another crucial part of long jumping is the take-off angle. Floating high in the air like many long jumpers only slowed Carl down and wasted his energy. To avoid this, Carl tried to keep his leap much closer to the ground than that of other jumpers. The danger in doing that, however, was that the momentum of his speed would naturally tend to spin his body into a somersault while he was in the air.

The way to avoid flipping was to get the legs working against the spin during the jump. And Carl did this by developing his famous double-hitch kick. When Carl was in the air, he looked like he was pretending to ride a bicycle. The 2-½ pedals that he went through in the air not only helped him keep his balance, they also brought his legs into proper position for a landing. This double hitch had to be practiced constantly until it was done by instinct. As Carl noted, "Once you hit the board, it's so quick you can't remember it." During his brief but wild 1-½-second trip through the air on a full-fledged long jump attempt, there would be no time to think about what he was supposed to be doing.

By the end of 1981, Carl had developed his skills so well that opponents were already starting to give up hope of beating him. That season, he took his first step on the road to catching a legend when he became the first man since Jesse Owens to win a national

Carl splashes down 26 feet, 8-½ inches away from the jumping board on his first jump during the qualifying rounds of the 1981 NCAA championships.

competition in both a track event—running—and a field event—jumping and throwing. While breaking into the top ranks of United States' 100-meter dashmen, Lewis established himself as the finest long jumper in the country. In the 1981 National Collegiate Athletic Association (NCAA) championships, Lewis was allowed to take nine long jumps. Although he decided to skip six of his nine attempts, he still ended up with the top three leaps in the competition!

Carl and Carol, who had followed her brother to the University of Houston a year later, could have made their school the top track power in the country, but it never turned out that way. Although Carl had been doing well in his studies as a communications major, he made the mistake of failing a history course. For that error, he was declared ineligible to compete in his junior year. Miffed, Lewis simply turned his back on the college athletic program. Although he continued to attend classes, Lewis was through running for Houston.

It was Lewis' good fortune to gain fame when the rules governing amateur athletes were relaxed to the point of being ridiculous. There were all kinds of ways that an athlete could accept money and still be considered an amateur, a person who competes in sport for fun and not for profit. When the word got out that Carl Lewis just might turn out to be one of the greatest trackmen of all time, many sponsors stepped forward to make deals with him. As a result, Carl could afford to live in an expensive house, hire Tellez as his own private coach, and still be eligible to compete in amateur track meets all over the country.

The more success Lewis had, particularly in the long jump, the higher he set his goals. When he announced that he was serious about going after Bob Beamon's Mexico City record, a great debate started among track and field experts about whether he had any chance of doing it. After all, wasn't that leap just a once-in-a-century fluke? Even the best long jumpers in the world seemed to think so. Since that 1968 record, no one had come close to 29 feet, 2-½ inches. In fact, they couldn't even reach 28 feet. In all of his attempts following his miracle jump, Beamon himself never topped 27 feet. The facts seemed to show he had somehow done the impossible.

But Carl and his coach didn't see it that way. After proving himself as the United States' best jumper and sprinter, Lewis needed a bigger challenge. Deep inside himself, he felt he was born to do something truly extraordinary. "God's given me the talent; I'm just trying to be patient with it," he said. Breaking Beamon's record would certainly be an extraordinary feat. Carl admitted he not only wanted to break it, he wanted to do it at sea level where the heavier air would make it more difficult. And, if pressed further, he would confess that he thought there was a 30-foot jump inside of him, just waiting to come out.

It did not take long for Carl to prove to a stunned track world that this was more than just idle talk. On July 24, 1982, in Indianapolis, Indiana, he roared down the long-jump runway and struck the takeoff board as close to the end as was humanly possible.

There were gasps from the crowd as Carl jetted over a seemingly unending stretch of carefully leveled sand. Just when it seemed he would crash out of the pit altogether, his legs finally came down near the back of the sand box. But the crowd's excitement turned to a groan, and Carl's look of triumph melted into anguish when an official signaled that he had fouled.

Many observers hotly disputed the call and pointed out that Carl had not disturbed the finely powdered substance spread just beyond the takeoff board to track any borderline fouls. But the official's call stood, and, under the rules of track and field, the jump would not even be measured. Carl had to watch as the evidence of what was probably the longest jump in history—even longer than Beamon's miracle leap of 1968—was raked away. Experts studying film of Lewis' Indianapolis jump concluded that Carl could have jumped 29-½ feet. Lewis himself thought he had landed closer to 30 feet.

Although that leap was never officially measured, it destroyed a myth about long jumping and showed that Beamon really had not reached the upper limit of human athletic ability. By breaking that mental barrier, Carl gave long jumpers new goals to shoot for. Larry Myricks, who had defeated Carl in the 1980 Olympic trials—the last man to defeat Lewis in an outdoor long jump—said Carl's jump "makes

This 1980 Olympic trials jump made Larry Myricks the last person to defeat Carl Lewis in an outdoor long jump.

it easier for all of us to go farther." Instead of hoping to reach 27 feet in competition, Myricks and other jumpers now started looking towards 28 feet.

For those skeptics who thought reports of Carl's Indianapolis jump were exaggerated, Lewis displayed a rash of 28-foot jumps. Included among those was a best of 28 feet, 10-¼ inches, which was within 5 inches of Bob Beamon's sacred ground. For his pioneering efforts in the event, Carl was named the 1982 Athlete of the Year by *Track and Field News*.

While he was still nipping at the heels of one legend, Carl took off after the other. He often thought of Jesse Owens and his historic trick of four track and field gold medals in a single Olympics. Having mastered one of Owens' events, the long jump, Carl

Jesse Owens wins the long jump in the 1936 Olympics, capturing the second of his four gold medals.

now turned his attention to the Buckeye Bullet's other specialty, the sprints. As in long jumping, Carl was willing to do whatever work was needed to make himself a successful sprinter, including scrapping his entire starting technique. At 6 feet, 2 inches, Carl was fairly tall for a sprinter, and tall sprinters generally do not have the quickness that smaller ones have in bursting out of the starting blocks. Lewis was even slower than most in getting into high gear. In a race as short and quick as the 100-meter dash, a bad start could mean defeat for even the fastest sprinter.

Carl worked hard on his coach's instructions to stay low to the ground as he drove out of his starting blocks. Once he had developed a respectable start, the rest was easy. He only had to practice his sprinting form, which has been called the smoothest in history. Even his competitors marveled at how high he could lift his knees and how every muscle seemed to be under control. In May 1983, when he roared through the 100 meters at Modesto, California, in 9.97 seconds—the fastest time ever recorded at sea level—Carl served warning that world sprint records were no safer than long-jump marks.

It might have been tempting for Lewis to stay with the 100 and the long jump and concentrate on breaking records. But the legend of Jesse Owens and his four gold medals goaded him on to another event. Besides winning the long jump and 100-meter dash in 1936, Owens had also picked up first places in the 400-meter (4 x 100) relay and the 200-yard dash. The relay would be no problem for Carl; his part would be almost identical to running a 100-meter race. That left the 200-meter dash as Carl's final challenge.

To match Owens' 1936 feat (above), Lewis had to take up a new event, the 200-meter dash.

If Lewis' dream of challenging Owen's mark had been a secret before, that secret was spilled in June 1983 when he added the 200 to his schedule of events at the Track Athletic Championship (TAC) meet. Carl had always run so effortlessly in the 100 that it seemed he might do well in the 200. The only questions were whether he could learn to sprint around a curve and if he had the endurance to finish strongly.

In just one race, Carl answered all of those questions when he blazed to a United States' record of 19.75, just off the world record of 19.72 set by Italy's Pietro Mennea. Only a foolish mistake by the inexperienced Lewis kept him from setting his first outdoor world record. Ten yards before the finish line, a joyful Lewis, realizing he would win the race, threw up his hands in joy. Veteran dashmen pointed out that his early celebration slowed him down and might have cost him a 10th of a second. Lee Evans, the retired world record holder at 400 meters, told of how many races he had won in the last three or four meters. He could not believe how often athletes would spoil years of preparation for a record by easing up before the end of a race.

In the same TAC meet, Carl also won the long jump and the 100-meter dash. In doing so, he became the first United States' athlete since 1886 to win the long jump and both sprints at a national championship meet.

Lewis stretches out for Beamon's world record but falls short with a leap of 28 feet, 10-¼ inches in this 1983 meet.

Now that he had proven it was possible to run well in all of those events at a single meet, all he needed to do before the 1984 Olympics was to test his overseas competiton. The chance came later that summer in the World Track and Field Championships at Helsinki, Finland. There Lewis discovered that his top competitors were all from the United States. In Helsinki, Lewis led a U.S.A. sweep of the top three places in both the long jump and the 100 meters. Instead of taxing himself with the 200-meter run, he chose to anchor—that is, run the final leg of—the 400-meter relay. Along with teammates Emmit King, Willie Gault, and Calvin Smith, Lewis sped along to a world record of 37.86. By this time, Carl's fame had spread beyond the pages of track magazines, and he was named Male Athlete of 1983 by the Associated Press.

While setting his sights on the 1984 Olympics in Los Angeles, Carl took time to make another effort at overhauling Beamon's record. In the Millrose Games at New York's Madison Square Garden in January 1984, Carl was suffering through one of his worst outings ever. In five weak jumps, the best he could manage was 27 feet, 2-¾ inches. Seeing his chance to beat Lewis at last, Larry Myricks flew 27 feet, 6 inches on his final try. Carl, however, had one more chance. This time he catapulted through the air for 28 feet, 10-¼ inches, which broke his own indoor long jump record by over 9 inches! Now it seemed just a matter of time before he would finally catch Beamon.

As the Olympics approached, Lewis found the challenges on the track were easy compared to what he faced *off* the track. Carl was not a natural celebrity. While his outgoing sister enjoyed the social scene, Carl, a very private person, had always held back. Carol once said she was the one who always tested new situations in life and then, when she found out they were safe, she would bring Carl along.

Although Carol could do some impressive feats of her own and was considered the United States' best woman long jumper, it was Carl who had to handle the publicity now. As much as he wanted to, it was no longer possible to stay to himself and enjoy quiet hobbies such as collecting crystal. He discovered just how little privacy he had when he received, among many pieces of fan mail, an overseas letter addressed only to "Carl Lewis, U.S.A." Carl's business agent also made sure that his client's name stayed near the headlines. It was he who declared that by the end of the Olympics, Lewis would be worth as much as multi-millionaire singer Michael Jackson!

Such statements did not endear Lewis to the public. The idea of track athletes planning to turn their records and medals into million-dollar money-making schemes just did not fit the country's traditional idea of the modest, dedicated sports hero. Criticism, much of it cruel, came from all directions. Some writers even sneered at Lewis' ability and wondered why he thought he was so great when he didn't even own an individual outdoor world record.

The more that the press built Lewis up as "King Carl" and "Superman IV," the more people expected of him. Not many individuals can relax and have fun living up to a larger-than-life buildup, and it was impossible for a shy, private person such as Carl. While Carl's agent planned to make him into a hot media star, Carl was not acting like one. He said he wanted to be known only as someone who was a nice guy and did his job in his own way.

Unfortunately for Carl, there was no way he could do things his own way *and* be considered a nice guy. On the track, Lewis often kept to himself when other athletes thought he should be more outgoing. But it was his actions at the end of a race that disturbed competitors even more. Besides costing him a world record, his habit of raising his arms in triumph before he hit the finish line seemed like hotdogging to some. So did his smiles of joy when he sometimes looked around to see how far behind his opponents were during the last meters of a race.

Those actions brought stinging criticism from the highly respected hurdler Edwin Moses who thought Carl was rubbing it in and not showing respect for his opponents. Lewis' chief rival in the long jump, Larry Myricks, confessed that his relationship with Carl was not the friendliest and that there would be some "serious celebrating" when Carl got beat.

Lewis argued that he wasn't intending to show off or belittle anyone. When he was happy, he couldn't help but show it. But his competitors were not convinced by his arguments, and Carl had to live with the criticism of not acting like a hero should.

Carl shrugged off all the controversy as best he could and geared up for the great Olympic challenge. While many of the 1984 Olympic events were hurt by the absence of the boycotting athletes from the Soviet Union and their allies, everyone admitted that the missing countries would have no effect on Carl's quest to match Owens' four gold medals. None of the Eastern bloc countries had an athlete who could come close to challenging for a gold medal in Carl's events. As the experts pointed out, the stiffest test on the way to the four golds would come well *before* the Olympics. To win a spot on the Olympic team in each of his events, Lewis would be going against the strongest sprinters and jumpers in the world, the United States' athletes.

34

By far the largest obstacle in Carl's way was the 100-meter dash at the United States' trials in Los Angeles in June 1984. The final race of the trials would possibly be the greatest collection of sprinters ever put together in one race and far more competitive than the Olympic final. To get a chance to compete in the Olympic 100, Carl needed to finish in the top three. One tiny lapse could ruin his chance.

Carl must have been thinking hard about the race because when he prepared to run one of the preliminary heats of the 100, he found he had not put on his shorts under his sweat pants! He had to wait while a friend nervously rushed to find Carl's uniform and get it to him in time. The man had to wave from the stands to attract Lewis' attention when security officers refused to allow him onto the field. After ducking into a stadium tunnel to slip on the shorts, Carl earned a spot in the finals.

Carl drew lane two for the finals. As he settled into his starting blocks, he was aware of the danger his dream was in. Calvin Smith, owner of the world record in this event—a 9.93 recorded at high altitude —was to his left in lane one. Brushing Carl's right shoulder was Emmit King, a member of the world-record 400-meter relay team and the 1983 NCAA 100-meter champ. The massive shoulders of Ron Brown filled lane four. Brown had passed up a rich pro football contract with the Los Angeles Rams for a chance to run in the Olympics. Lane five belonged to Mel Lattany, whose best time of 9.96 topped anything Carl had ever done. Harvey Glance, veteran of the 1976 Olympics, crouched in lane six. The last two lanes were given to the NCAA's most recent dash champions. Kirk Baptiste, the college 200-meter king, seemed to be improving with every race. Sam Graddy, the NCAA 100-meter champ, was out in lane eight, where he could sneak past Lewis without Carl ever seeing him. Only three of these eight record-holding sprinters would qualify for the Olympic 100.

At the crack of the gun, eight pairs of legs churned into action. Carl started well and stayed in the middle of the tightly-packed wall of runners. Gradually, he pulled away from the field, clocking a 10.06 time running into a wind. Graddy finished second, and Brown edged the rest for third place. The competition had been so fierce that the world record holder, Calvin Smith, did not qualify for the Olympic 100.

Carl's first place finish automatically gave him a spot on the 400-meter relay team, and he had no problem in qualifying for the 200-meter dash or the long jump. If he could stand up to the pressure of the Olympics and the grueling series of preliminary heats, Lewis was almost certain to gain the heights that only Jesse Owens had reached.

What a relief! Carl wins the 100-meter dash in the 1984 U.S.A. Olympic trials. The race was so close that Emmit King, who appears to be right behind Carl, finished fifth and missed a spot on the U.S.A. team.

Olympic fans throughout the world were reminded of the legend
Carl Lewis was chasing when Gina Hemphill, Jesse Owens'
granddaughter, was chosen to run the Olympic torch into the
Los Angeles Coliseum.

In 1936, 22-year-old Jesse Owens had entered hostile territory. The Olympics were being held in Berlin, Germany, under the watchful eye of Nazi dictator Adolph Hitler. The Games were to be a showcase for the Nazi claim that the European race was far superior to any other people in the world. But it was a black athlete, Owens, who dominated the events.

Jesse had taken advantage of teammate Ralph Metcalf's slow start to sprint to victory in the 100-meter dash. Metcalf finished second to Owens' world-record-tying 10.2. In the long jump, Jesse could easily have been unnerved by a misunderstanding. He simply ran through the pit on his warmup only to learn that the competition had actually begun. When that attempt was declared a foul, Owens started jumping poorly. But after a chat with his friendly chief competitor from Germany, Owens pulled himself together for a leap of 26 feet, 5 inches.

Not only did that win the gold medal, it also stood as a world record for 25 years! After that, Owens had breezed to victory with an Olympic record in the 200 meters and a world record in the 400-meter relay. It was Carl Lewis' job to match that incredible speed and athletic talent.

Just as it had been in the Olympic trials, the 100-yard dash would be Carl's most difficult challenge.

The world's fastest male jogs with Evelyn Ashford, the world's fastest female. Ashford won the women's 100-meter dash at the 1984 Olympics and set a world record of 10.76 in the event later that month.

It is difficult to relax when an instant's hesitation can drop a runner from first to last, but Carl knew that the key to winning the race was in relaxing so his body could run smoothly.

After routinely working his way to the finals, Carl stared down the track to his first gold medal, 100 meters away. This time, he had drawn lane seven, two lanes away from Sam Graddy, his most dangerous medal threat. Graddy, settling into lane five, seemed hot-wired for quick starts. He was fast enough so that Lewis could not afford to let him get too much of a lead.

As if to show his critics that he was still going to do things his way, Carl had come to the Olympics wearing his hair in a very distinctive, square, brush cut. He didn't need a special haircut to attract attention, however, as everyone in the stadium was watching Carl Lewis.

At the starter's signal, the sprinters reared up for the start. When the gun sounded, Sam Graddy shot out of the blocks with the suddenness of a gust of wind shattering a pane of glass. Carl got off to a decent start, but it was taking him some time to reach the speed of the shorter Graddy. At the halfway point, he was still no better than third. To inexperienced spectators, it looked as if Carl would lose.

But while other runners had reached top speed and

were trying to hold it for the last 50 meters, Lewis was still accelerating. Graddy fought furiously to hold his lead and thought he might have a chance to win when Carl still had not caught him at 80 meters. But then came the optical illusion. Lewis shot by so quickly that it seemed he had reserved an extra kick for the end. Actually, he had just maintained the tremendous speed he had finally built up to while the other sprinters had begun to slow slightly.

Carl finished so strongly that his time of 9.99 was .2 of a second faster than the second-place Graddy, who had held off Canada's Ben Johnson for the silver medal. In a 100-meter race, .2 of a second is a decisive margin of defeat. It was not the usual Lewis expression of joy that fans saw at the end of the race. Carl looked more like an outlaw who had just escaped from a close brush with a posse. He seemed just plain relieved that the event was over.

Lewis put in his toughest day of Olympic work on August 6, 1984. As he prepared for the long-jump finals that evening, he was starting to feel the effects of all the activity that day. He had already run two heats of the 200-meter dash, a tiring race for him, in order to qualify for the semifinals. He had also done the preliminary long jumps that had qualified him for the final. Coach Tellez had been worried about this day. Knowing how much long jumping saps an athlete's legs, he knew that Carl needed to qualify on his first jumps to ease the strain on his legs. Fortunately, Carl had done that.

Now a packed crowd was looking for Carl to shift his sights away from Jesse Owens and on to Bob Beamon's record. Little did they know a tricky swirling wind and the hurried pace of Carl's day would make his effort futile. Nevertheless, Lewis sped down the runway to give it his best shot. Hitting his takeoff spot well, he soared 28 feet, ¼ inch, the second-longest jump in Olympic history.

In that one brief instant, the long-jump competition was over. Carl tried a second jump but stepped over the end of the board for a foul. He would be allowed four more jumps. But when he pulled on his sweat pants, he decided that he was probably through for the night. His leg had felt a little sore after his second jump, and he remembered his coach's warning about how taxing a single long jump could be. As he saw the competition falling far short of his mark, he realized that conditions were far from ideal for breaking the record. So knowing that he had probably clinched first place with his first jump, he passed his final attempts in order to save himself for the events that remained.

When the crowd realized what Carl was doing, they began booing him. They felt they had paid good money to see him at least try to reach Beamon's mark, but they had misjudged Carl's personality. They had come to see Carl Lewis, the entertainer. But despite Carl's position as a star, he wasn't an entertainer. Lewis was an athlete, and he was after only one thing: four gold medals. If there were world records to be set, he would deal with them later.

As it turned out, only one other jumper came within a foot of Carl's first jump. Now it was two gold medals down and two to go.

Lewis cruised through his semifinal heat of the 200-meter dash in an excellent time of 20.27. Based on the few times he had run the event, the 200 seemed to be Carl's best race. Among track experts, the only suspense in the race was whether or not he would break the world record.

In the 200-meter dash, runners begin by running on a curve of the track and then finish on a straightaway. Carl had been having some trouble getting a smooth, relaxed stride on the curve portion of the race, and he wanted to master that problem in the finals. As he bent down into his starting blocks, he made up his mind to do the best curve-running of his life.

Carl finishes his closest Olympic race, the 200-meter dash, with a glance at fast-closing Kirk Baptiste in lane one (*not pictured*). The world record holder in the event, Pietro Mennea (551), strains but can't come close to catching Lewis.

Another United States' runner, Thomas Jefferson, got the best start in the race, but Lewis quickly passed him. Charging around the curve as he had never done before, Carl had already stretched out to a comfortable lead when he reached the straightaway. Since Carl's finish had always been the best part of his race, it looked like he was on his way to a world record. Carl, however, had used up too much energy on the curve. As he neared the tape, it was obvious that he was not pulling away. In fact, he was being caught by the fast-closing Kirk Baptiste, the third U.S.A. runner in the race.

Three down and one to go! Knowing that the incredible strain he has been under is almost over, Carl savors his 200-meter win.

Lewis joins teammates Kirk Baptiste (*left*) and Thomas Jefferson (*right*) in a celebration of their sweep of the top three places in the 200-meter dash.

Fortunately, Carl got to the finish tape before Baptiste reached him. Although his time of 19.80 was within .07 of a world record, Carl's margin of victory was less in the 200 than it had been in the 100. His fast start had nearly been a fatal mistake, and Carl was glad he had not spent any more of his energy back at the long-jump pit.

Even legends can't do it all on their own. Jesse Owens (*left*) poses with the men who helped him win the 400-meter relay: (*left to right*) Ralph Metcalfe, Foy Draper, and Frank Wykoff.

It would have been better show business if Carl had been pushed by tough competition when he tried to win the medal that would link him forever with Jesse Owens. But everyone knew the 400-meter relay was going to be a cakewalk for the U.S. team. After all, it was almost certain that four of the five fastest men in the race would be running for the U.S.A. Even if they had sloppy baton exchanges, Carl and his teammates would still win. Only a dropped baton could beat them.

From his spot on the far curve of the track, Lewis watched his teammates carry his gold medal hopes in their hands. While there wasn't a chance of them being outsprinted, his medal wouldn't be safe until he could feel the baton firmly in his fingers. Sam Graddy led off and raced around the first curve towards Ron Brown. Brown then pounded down the

World 100-meter record holder Calvin Smith hands off the baton to team anchor Carl Lewis.

Lewis blazes down the final straightaway and (*opposite*), with gold medal number four safely around his neck, enjoys a ride from his relay teammates.

backstretch and handed off to Calvin Smith. As he zeroed in on Lewis, Smith opened up a large lead.

None of the handoffs were perfect, and Lewis made the risky move of switching the baton from one hand to the other during his run. But the exchanges were smooth enough to let the speedsters do their work. Carl Lewis flew across the finish line in a time of 37.83. The four gold medals were now his, and it was especially satisfying to cap his pursuit of the Jesse Owens' legend with a world-record time in the relay.

The ease with which Carl had captured his four golds made it seem as though his quest had never been in danger. But the following track season showed why even a great athlete like Lewis had felt such tremendous pressure. Intending to top the Beamon long-jump record in 1985, Carl instead strained a muscle in his right leg during a May 18 competition. That minor problem kept him from even making the finals of the USA-Mobil Outdoor Track and Field Championships and forced him to postpone his world-record dreams for another year.

While Carl's Olympic success did attract some strange offers—for instance, he had never played organized football or basketball but was drafted by the Dallas Cowboys and the Chicago Bulls—criticism of his aloof attitude during the Olympics slowed the expected flood of commercial offers to just a trickle. But whether or not he turns out to be a financial success, Carl Lewis has proven that he deserves to rate with the greatest athletes of all time. He has chased down one of the track's greatest legends and has come within a sliver of catching another.

Sometimes Lewis talks of trying other challenges like the 400 meters or the hurdles. But the time is fast approaching when he will no longer be chasing legends. Instead, he will be challenging the brave souls who are trying to catch *him!*

CARL LEWIS : LEGEND CHASER

	1984 Olympics	World Record
100-Meter Dash	9.99 seconds CARL LEWIS U.S.A. August 4, 1984	9.93 seconds Calvin Smith U.S.A. July 3, 1983
200-Meter Dash	19.80 seconds CARL LEWIS U.S.A. August 8, 1984	19.73 seconds Pietro Mennea Italy · September 12, 1979
Long Jump	28 feet, ¼ inch CARL LEWIS U.S.A. August 6, 1984	29 feet, 2-½ inches Bob Beamon U.S.A. October 18, 1968
400-Meter Relay	37.83 seconds Sam Graddy Ron Brown Calvin Smith CARL LEWIS August 11, 1984	see *1984 Olympics*

U.S.A. Record	Olympic Record	1936 Olympics
see *World Record*	9.95 seconds Jim Hines U.S.A. October 14, 1968	10.3 seconds Jesse Owens U.S.A. August 3, 1936
19.75 seconds CARL LEWIS U.S.A. June 19, 1983	see *1984 Olympics*	20.7 seconds Jesse Owens U.S.A. August 5, 1936
see *World Record*	see *World Record*	26 feet, 5-¼ inches Jesse Owens U.S.A. August 4, 1936
see *1984 Olympics*	see *1984 Olympics*	39.8 seconds Jesse Owens Ralph Metcalfe Foy Draper Frank Wykoff August 9. 1936

	Carl Lewis' Personal Best	Jesse Owens' Personal Best
100-Meter Dash	9.97 seconds	10.2 seconds
200-Meter Dash	19.75 seconds	20.3 seconds
Long Jump	28 feet, 10-¾ inches	26 feet, 8-¼ inches
400-Meter Relay	37.83 seconds	39.8 seconds

ACKNOWLEDGMENTS: The photographs are reproduced through the courtesy of: pp. 1, 9, 12, 14, 21, 28, 37, 40, 45, 46, 47, 49, 50, 51, 53, AP/Wide World Photos; pp. 2, 7, 25, 26, 30, 38, 48, UPI/Bettmann Archive; p. 6, 3M Company; pp. 10 (left and right), 11, Tuskegee Institute Archives. Cover photograph © 1984 by Robert Long/LPI.

56